VANGUARD SER...

EDITOR: MARTIN WI...

US HALF-TRACKS of WORLD WAR II

Text and colour plates by

STEVEN J. ZALOGA

OSPREY PUBLISHING LONDON

Published in 1983 by
Osprey Publishing Ltd
Member company of the George Philip Group
12–14 Long Acre, London WC2E 9LP
© Copyright 1983 Osprey Publishing Ltd
Reprinted 1984, 1985 (twice), 1988

British Library Cataloguing in Publication Data

Zaloga, Steven J.
  US half tracks of World War II.—(Vanguard; 31)
  1. United States. *Army*—History
  2. Half-track vehicles, Military—History
  I. Title   II. Series
  623.74′7   UG446.5

  ISBN 0-85045-481-6

Filmset in Great Britain
Printed in Hong Kong

Acknowledgements
The Author would like to extend his thanks to James
Loop; George Balin; Martha Cedar, White-Volvo
archivist; Paul White, Still Photos Branch, National
Archives; and Leroy Jackson, Modern Military
Branch, National Archives, for their kind assistance in
the preparation of this book.

The Requirement

Ancestor of the armoured half-track was the T5 artillery prime mover, like this vehicle of Battery B, 68th Field Artillery towing a 75mm M1A1 field howitzer.

The full combat potential of tanks can be realised only when they are skilfully employed in conjunction with the other fighting arms, particularly the infantry. The failure of tanks in their initial combat debut at Flers in 1916 underscored their limitations in holding on to hard-won terrain against vigorous enemy infantry counter-attacks. A consequence of French and American experience with tank-infantry combinations in 1918 was the relegation of tanks to the infantry support rôle. Tank-infantry co-operation could thus be assured, since the slow 'infantry tank' moved hardly faster than a walking rifleman. More far-sighted theoreticians in Germany and Britain realised that this rôle did not take full advantage of the potential mobility of the tank; but the crucial dilemma was how to ensure infantry co-operation with tanks which *could* easily outpace walking infantrymen. The solution was the mechanisation of the infantry to permit them to move along with the tanks. This

was a seminal factor in the development of modern *blitzkreig* warfare.

The development of mechanised infantry by the US Army was belated, and the key piece of equipment for these new tactics, the armoured half-track personnel carrier, was born of the initiatives of the Cavalry Department, not the Infantry. The Ordnance Department had shown interest in the Citroën-Kegresse semi-track designs since the 1920s, and developed a number of derivatives in the 1930s as unarmoured prime movers for the artillery. The main advantage of half-tracks over conventional lorries or fully-tracked prime movers was that they had better mobility in rough terrain than lorries, yet were not as expensive, complicated or as difficult to maintain as fully-tracked prime movers.

In the 1930s, the Cavalry's experience with armoured scout cars convinced them of the need for a vehicle with better cross-country mobility

3

and suitable both for scouting and towing artillery. An M2A1 Scout Car was successfully converted to half-track configuration in 1938 as the T7; but its mobility was restricted by lack of powered front wheels, and it had inadequate internal stowage capacity. A second effort was sponsored by the Mechanized Cavalry Board in December 1939, eventually resulting in the White Motor Company T14 'Halftrack Armored Car'. By the time that the T14 prototypes became available the US Army was in the throes of massive re-organisation, including the birth of the new Armored Force. The T14 was immediately accepted for service use in September 1940 as the 'Halftrack Armored Car M2'. Two further types were also contemplated, the 'Halftrack Personnel Carrier M3', which had a longer hull and greater seating capacity; and the 'Halftrack Mortar Carrier M4', which was similar to the M2 but mounted an 81mm mortar. The Autocar Company was the successful low bidder for the original half-track manufacturing contract; but with war brewing in Europe and the Pacific, the Army prudently extended production to the White Motor Company and Diamond T Motor Company.

The new half-tracks were desperately needed by the new armoured infantry regiments. The 6th Infantry was the first regiment to be slated for mechanisation on 15 July 1940, even before the M2 had been accepted for service use. During the course of 1940 and 1941, 14 additional regiments were called up and mechanised, with more scheduled to follow. The newly formed armoured division consisted of two armoured regiments and a single armoured infantry regiment. The armoured infantry regiment required 230 half-tracks, and each of the armoured regiments a further 100, for a grand total of 733 half-tracks in

Half-Track Production during World War II

Type	Manufacturer	1941	1942	1943	1944	Total
M2	White, Autocar	3,565	4,735	3,115		11,415
M2A1	White, Autocar			987	656	1,643
M3	White, Autocar, Diamond T	1,859	4,959	5,681		12,499
M3A1	White, Autocar, Diamond T			2,037	825	2,862
M5	IHC		152	4,473		4,625
M5A1	IHC			1,859	1,100	2,959
M9	IHC			2,026		2,026
M9A1	IHC			1,407		1,407
57mm GMC T48	Diamond T		50	912		962
75mm GMC M3, M3A1	Autocar	86	1,350	766		2,202
75mm HMC T30	White		500			500
105mm HMC T19	Diamond T		324			324
M13 MGMC	White			1,103		1,103
M14 MGMC	IHC		5	1,600		1,605
M16 MGMC	White			2,323	554	2,877
M17 MGMC	IHC			400	600	1,000
T10 MGMC	White				110	110
T28E1 CGMC	Autocar		80			80
M15 MGMC	Autocar			680		680
M15A1 MGMC	Autocar			1,052	600	1,652
81mm MMC M4	White		572			572
81mm MMC M4A1	White			600		600
81mm MMC M21	White				110	110

an armoured division under the 1942 Table of Organization and Equipment (TO&E). Besides the basic carrier versions, there were a wide variety of specialised gun carrier types (see later chapter).

The M2 half-track closely resembled the new M3A1 Scout Car in general configuration, with the obvious exception of the tracks. It had capacity for ten men, and was cramped in the centre section due to the presence of a large stowage box on either side, which could be reached from either interior or exterior doors. The vehicle's machine gun armament was mounted on a skate ring which ran around the whole upper inside edge of the hull. Because of the skate ring, there was no rear exit door. The M2 half-track was intended for use as a command vehicle, reconnaissance vehicle, prime mover for artillery, and as a carrier for mortar and machine gun squads. It was too small to carry a full infantry squad.

The M3 half-track was identical to the M2 half-track as far back as the partition behind the driver. The M3 had a longer hull to permit

The US Army's first experience with half-tracks came during the summer wargames of 1941. This M2 belonged to the 14th Field Artillery during the September 1941 manoeuvres in Louisiana. Like many armoured vehicles headquartered at Ft. Knox, this vehicle is marked with the Armored Force insignia of the time, a white star on a red circle with a pale blue centre—the reverse of the Army Air Corps insignia of the time. With the outbreak of war, this gave way to the more familiar white or yellow star.

seating for a driver and 12 men; and unlike the M2, it had a rear access door, and lacked the large interior stowage bins. Instead of the skate ring, the main machine gun on an M3 was carried on a pedestal mount, and further pintle socket mounts could be attached elsewhere for additional machine guns. The basic rôle of the M3 was to transport rifle squads, but it was also used as an armoured utility vehicle to carry ammunition for armoured field artillery batteries, as an unarmed armoured ambulance, and to perform light maintenance tasks. In the latter rôle, a special version was built with a winch in front which was powered off the engine's drive train. This was fitted in place of the usual roller bumper. Although small numbers of M2s were built with winches, the M3 version was by far the most common winch type.

Capt. Paulick and Lt. Gioia of the 601st Tank Destroyer Bn. confer in front of an M2 command half-track near El Guettar, Tunisia, 23 March 1943. It was on this day that the battalion, in support of the 1st Infantry Division, beat back a furious German tank attack, losing 21 of its 31 75mm GMC M3 tank destroyers, like the one in the background, but causing the Germans even more severe losses. (US Signal Corps)

Half-Tracks in Combat

The M2 and M3 half-tracks were used in the autumn 1941 Tennessee and Louisiana wargames. Their combat debut came months later in the Philippines with the Provisional Tank Group, which had 46 half-tracks. These were used mainly in command and general utility rôles, and were much preferred to the Bren carriers otherwise used by the unit[1]. The Philippines fighting uncovered many technical shortcomings in the half-track, especially in the suspension, and these were reported to the Ordnance Department by radio before the fall of Bataan. The Provisional

Tank Group officers were critical not only of the fragility of the suspension, but of the lack of thick armour and overhead armour cover. Although the Ordnance Department initiated immediate modification programmes to correct the suspension difficulties, the lack of overhead armour was to remain a controversial feature of the M2 and M3 half-track. Prototypes of half-tracks with overhead cover were built and tested, but Ordnance felt that the added weight excessively degraded the automotive performance of the vehicle.

The M2 and M3 half-tracks played a prominent rôle in the fighting in Tunisia in 1942 and 1943 with the 6th Armored Infantry (1st Armored Division). They were not particularly popular, earning the sobriquet 'Purple Heart Boxes'—a grim reference to the US Army decoration for combat wounds. When Gen. Omar Bradley asked a veteran if the half-track's armour could be penetrated by German machine gun fire, the rifleman sarcastically quipped: 'No sir, it does not. As a matter of fact bullets generally only come in one side and rattle around a bit.' (In fact, the armour of the half-track gave reasonably good

---

[1] These had been impressed into service after a freighter bound for Malaya was forced by the outbreak of the war to dock in the Philippines.

protection against 7.62mm AP ammunition at ranges over 200 metres.) Nor were the regimental or divisional commanders any more enamoured of the half-track. In their postmortem on the Tunisian campaign, they condemned the half-track as wasteful of road space and manpower, and recommended that armoured infantry be carried in trucks instead. They complained: 'Experience to date has not justified the carrying of infantry in an expensive armoured vehicle which is difficult to maintain and which in protection . . . is practically nil against bombing and artillery.' Nevertheless, Bradley disagreed: 'The American half-track was a competent and dependable contrivance. Its bad name resulted from the inexperience of our troops, who attempted to use it for too many things.'

In the wake of the US Army's painful acquisition of battlefield experience with the new tools of mechanised warfare in Tunisia, technical improvements were incorporated into the half-track, and the armoured infantry was re-organised. Ordnance refused to consider increasing the armour, which was $\frac{1}{4}$in. overall with a $\frac{1}{2}$in. windshield. Overheating of engines in Tunisia led to the addition of a radiator surge tank; and a dual air intake air cleaner was installed to reduce dust and sand ingestion problems. Heavier bogie springs and a heavier spring for the rear idler were found to correct remaining suspension problems. Neither the skate ring nor pedestal mounts for machine guns were deemed acceptable from combat experience, which led to the adoption of the M49 machine gun mount. This pulpit mount was added to the right front of the vehicle beside the driver, and permitted easier use of machine guns against aircraft. These changes resulted in the new M2A1 and M3A1 half-tracks. Some older

During the fighting at Kasserine Pass, several half-tracks like this M3 were lost to the Afrika Korps, which impressed them into their own service. This vehicle still has its yellow American star as well as an improvised German cross. (ECPA)

While Maj.Gen. George S. Patton commanded the 1st Armored Corps at the Desert Training Center in the US in 1942, he used this 'customised' M3 command half-track. This vehicle is shown as Plate A1, as it appeared after its insignia had been added.

vehicles were later rebuilt with some of these features, notably the M49 pulpit.

The 1943 re-organisation of the armoured divisions was mainly intended to correct the imbalance of tanks and infantry in favour of the infantry. In place of two armoured regiments and one armoured infantry regiment, the new 'light' configuration armoured divisions had three armoured infantry battalions (AIB) and three tank battalions. On the face of it, this would not seem to be much of an increase in armoured infantry, since the old armoured infantry regiment also had three battalions. However, the new 1943 AIBs were larger and better armed. The 1942 armoured infantry rifle company had only three platoons with a single 37mm anti-tank gun per platoon. The new 1943 company had four platoons, the addition being an anti-tank platoon with three 57mm guns. Moreover, rifle squads under the 1942 organisation had only 11 men, while under the 1943 organisation they had 12 men like a conventional 'straight-leg' infantry squad. The 1942 company had 178 men and 17 half-tracks, while the 1943 company had 20 half-tracks and 251 men. Another important addition was the deployment of one new M1 2.35in. Rocket Launcher (bazooka) per squad to further enhance the anti-tank firepower of the company.

These changes took time to implement and did not affect the 2nd and 3rd Armored Divisions, which kept a modified form of the 1942 'heavy'

division configuration; and 1st Armored Division did not completely change to the 1943 TO&E until June 1944. The 1943 changes also marked a decided shift in the US Army towards the M3 half-track. The lack of a rear door on the M2 was a definite hindrance, and it did not offer as much interior stowage capacity as the M3. This shift in preference manifested itself in the changing production totals from 1942 and 1943.

The 41st Armored Infantry Regiment's fight on Sicily did not end the disparagement of the half-track. The 2nd Armored Division's commander, Gen. Hugh Gaffey, again fumed that the 'gypsy caravan' of half-tracks should be replaced with 2½-ton trucks. However, Col. Sidney Hinds firmly opposed the idea. Hinds and fellow infantry supporters pointed out that the divisional commanders did not appreciate the importance of armoured half-tracks in sustained, fast-moving combat. Armoured infantry could fight without the heavy encumbrance of their full personal kit, trusting that it would be available when needed in the half-track. They could rely on half-tracks to follow them anywhere, while trucks could hardly be expected to cross the sort of terrain traversed by tanks. The armour, even if thin, meant that half-tracks could deliver their infantry much closer to their objectives even under intense infantry fire, thereby reducing casualties. As a home-away-from-home, the half-track soon became a storehouse for ammunition, supplies, and the usual collection of knick-knacks that not only increased the firepower of an infantry squad, but sustained its morale. It is quite interesting to note that Maj. Gen. Lesley McNair, head of Army Ground Forces and the chief advocate of austere, interchangeable units, endorsed the ideas of men like Hinds even in exception to his strict rules. McNair backed the 1943 organisation in spite of the higher expense and maintenance demands of half-track infantry units. This would prove to be fortunate during the fighting in France and Germany in 1944–45.

Organisation and Tactics

The Army planned to raise 48 battalions of armoured infantry for attachment to the 16 armoured divisions, plus an additional 20 battalions which could be used to strengthen the armoured divisions or be used independently. This latter idea was dropped, and of the 66 AIBs formed during the war all but one of the non-divisional battalions were disbanded prior to the campaigns of 1944.

An Armored Infantry Battalion consisted of five companies: three rifle companies, a headquarters company and a service company. The headquarters company had a battalion HQ (four jeeps, two half-tracks); a company HQ platoon consisting of a maintenance section (a jeep, a half-track with a winch, and a one-ton trailer), an administrative, mess and supply section (a 2½-ton truck and trailer), an HQ section (a jeep and a half-track); a battalion reconnaissance platoon (five machine gun-armed jeeps and a half-track); a mortar platoon (three M4 or M21 81mm half-tracks and an M3 half-track); a machine gun platoon (three half-tracks); and an assault gun platoon (three M7 Priest 105mm self-propelled howitzers, two half-tracks and four M10 ammunition trailers). The service company had 14 2½-ton trucks, 14 one-ton trailers, two ¾-ton trucks, three jeeps, one half-track, a 6-ton wrecker and an M32 ARV. The rifle companies, as described earlier, had three rifle platoons, an anti-tank platoon and an HQ platoon.

Each rifle platoon was made up of five half-tracks, each carrying a squad. There were three rifle squads, one carrying the platoon commander (a lieutenant), plus a light machine gun squad and a mortar squad. The rifle squads were composed of 12 men—a squad leader (sergeant), an assistant squad leader (corporal), nine riflemen (privates) and a driver. Each member of the squad was armed with an M1 Garand .30cal. rifle, though often one sharpshooter was attached to the

The M2 half-track was too cramped inside, leading many units to add a large stowage bin to the rear. Here, an M2 is used on scout duty near Venafro, Italy, in December 1943. (US Signal Corps)

This interior view of an M3 half-track gives some idea of the stowage. At the extreme left is a set of signalling flags: since only the platoon commanders had radios, inter-vehicle communications were by hand or flag signals. On the fuel tank is a bazooka, and behind it is taped the instruction sheet for flag signalling. In the benches below, the seats have been raised to show the stowage of canned rations and ammunition inside. The .30cal. Browning air-cooled machine gun is mounted on an M25 truck pedestal. To the right, M1 Garand rifles are evident, and outside is a rack full of mines. The tubular projections along the upper lip of the side walls are attachment points for the metal ribs of the canvas tilt that could be fitted in bad weather.

The distinctive feature of the new M3A1 half-track was the M49 pulpit mount, usually occupied by the vehicle's squad leader. This particular vehicle, 'Daring', belonged to D Co., 1st Bn., 41st Armored Infantry Regt., 2nd Armored Div. and is seen passing through Cantigny, France, 31 August 1944. The 2nd Armored Division regularly marked its half-tracks and tanks with prominent tactical numbers in yellow paint, as is the case here with 'D-9'. (US Signal Corps)

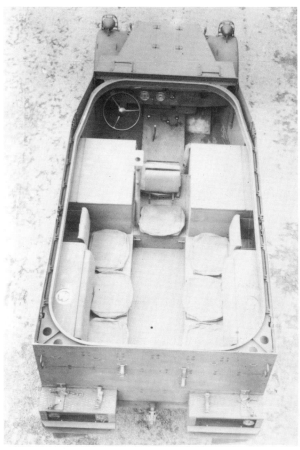

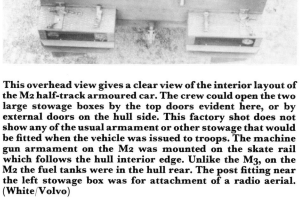

This overhead view gives a clear view of the interior layout of the M2 half-track armoured car. The crew could open the two large stowage boxes by the top doors evident here, or by external doors on the hull side. This factory shot does not show any of the usual armament or other stowage that would be fitted when the vehicle was issued to troops. The machine gun armament on the M2 was mounted on the skate rail which follows the hull interior edge. Unlike the M3, on the M2 the fuel tanks were in the hull rear. The post fitting near the left stowage box was for attachment of a radio aerial. (White/Volvo)

This overhead view provides a good comparison of the M3 half-track personnel carrier. The greater seating capacity of the M3 is quite evident, as is the ample stowage behind the rear seats. (White/Volvo)

platoon leader's half-track and was armed with a bolt-action M1903 Springfield .30cal. sniper rifle. The driver in all armoured infantry half-tracks was armed with an M3 .45cal. 'grease gun'. Besides individual arms, the rifle squads each had an M1 or M9 bazooka, and the vehicle-mounted .30cal. M1917A1 Browning machine gun. The platoon leader's half-track was authorised a .50cal. Browning M2HB machine gun instead of the lighter .30cal. weapon. The machine guns could be dismounted from the vehicle, and ground-mount tripods were carried.

The standard operating procedure (SOP) usually called for the squad leader to sit in the left seat of the cab, a rifleman/assistant driver in the centre and the driver to the right. On the M3A1 and M2A1 the squad leader was responsible for firing the pulpit-mounted machine gun. The assistant squad leader was assigned the left rear corner seat, while the bazooka team sat in the third and fourth seats on the right side, with the fifth rear corner seat opposite the assistant squad leader vacant. When the vehicle machine gun was dismounted the machine gun was crewed by a team of three riflemen consisting of the assistant driver/rifleman and the two other riflemen in the right side of the half-track. The other riflemen assigned specific tasks were the two in the front left seats, who served as squad scouts.

The light machine gun squad also consisted of 12 men: the driver, a squad leader and assistant leader, two gunners, two ammo-handlers and five riflemen. The riflemen were armed with M1

RA PD 18608

Interior view of M5 half-track (International Harvester): (A) Forward tarp mount (B) Right fuel tank (C) Pintle mount for machine gun (D) Middle tarp mount (E) Forward handle (F) Front floor plate (G) Rifle rack (H) Rifle rack (I) Forward stowage compartment (J) Rear handles (K) Centre stowage compartment (L) Rear tarp (tilt) mount (M) Rear rifle rack (N) Rear stowage compartment (right) (O) rear left rifle rack (P) Rear handles (Q) Seat backrest (R) Seat cushion (S) Rifle rack (T) Mounting point (U) Forward seat backrest (V) Left fuel tank (W) Attachment point (X) Forward attachment point.

Garand rifles, while the rest of the squad (with the obvious exception of the driver) were armed with M1 or M2 carbines. The light machine gun squad had a single M2HB .50cal. machine gun mounted on the M49 pulpit, plus two .30cal. Browning light machine guns, mounted on either side of the rear in pintle mounts. The mortar squad had only eight men: a squad leader, driver, two riflemen, two gunners and two ammo-handlers. As in the case of the light machine gun squad, carbines were used by all the squad members but the riflemen and driver. The basic squad weapon was a 60mm M2 mortar, which was usually fired from a dismounted position.

The 1943 TO&E called for the use of M3s or M3A1s by a rifle company. If the unit was still saddled with some M2s or M2A1s, these were usually used by the mortar squad or by the HQ

Interior view of M9A1 half-track (International Harvester): (A) M49 ring mount (B) Ring mount support attachment (C) Ring mount support (E) Machine gun pintle mount (F) Seat backrest (G) Cushion (H) Handle (I) Side handle (J) Right fuel tank (K) Floor board (L) Right stowage frame (M) Left stowage frame (N) Left handle (O) Left fuel tank (P) Bazooka attachment (Q) Attachment lug (R) Seat backrest (S) Forward attachment assembly (T) Left stowage bin.

RA PD 18611

A squad of 'armoured doughs' in action near Bubenorbis, Germany, on 17 April 1945. This squad from C Co., 61st Armd. Inf. Bn., 10th Armd. Div. have dismounted from their M2A1 (winch), with the squad leader in the lead. (US Signal Corps)

and AT companies. Needless to say, the official equipment tables above cannot begin to describe the actual firepower of an armoured infantry battalion in action. In keeping with the usual infantry penchant for walking off with anything not firmly bolted to the ground, rifle squads often had more machine guns than allotted. By trading with other units the much-prized tanker's jackets, Thompson sub-machine guns and BARs could often be obtained. Although armoured infantry companies frequently captured German small arms, they were sometimes discouraged from using captured automatic weapons, particularly the MG34 and MG42 machine guns. During night battles or in confused urban fighting, the distinctive sound of the German machine guns could make the user an unintended target of the fire of other rifle squads. One of the most appreciated German weapons was the Panzerfaust, though care had to be taken firing these, particularly from the confines of a half-track.

One of the least appreciated weapons was the US Army's M1 57mm anti-tank gun. This was largely ineffective against German tanks like the Panther and Tiger, and only marginally effective against the old PzKpfw IV. Some units, like the armoured infantry battalions of the 4th Armored Division, simply 'lost' their guns and converted the anti-tank platoons into additional rifle platoons; dealing with tanks was left to the accompanying Shermans. Though rarely used in many AIBs, the 57mm anti-tank gun could prove to be a useful weapon for clearing buildings of observers or snipers. In some battalions the anti-tank platoon was so seldom committed to combat in its intended rôle that it was saddled with other tasks, such as clearing minefields or laying treadway bridges across small streams.

Armoured infantry battalions were usually committed to action in conjunction with one of the armoured division's tank battalions to form a 'Combat Command'. The battalion worked in close co-ordination with the tanks. The infantry would keep the tanks free from German infantry and secure captured ground, while the tanks provided the shock power of the attack, and anti-tank protection. The official tasks of the armoured infantry were set down in FM 17-42 as:

'(a) Follow a tank attack to wipe out remaining enemy resistance.
(b) Seize and hold terrain gained by tanks.
(c) Attack and seize terrain favourable for tank attack.
(d) Form, in conjunction with artillery and tank destroyers, a base of fire for tank attack.
(e) Attack in conjunction with tanks.
(f) Clear lanes through minefields in conjunction with engineers.
(g) Protect tank units in bivouac, on the march, in assembly areas and at rallying points.
(h) Force a river crossing.
(i) Seize a bridgehead
(j) Establish and reduce obstacles.

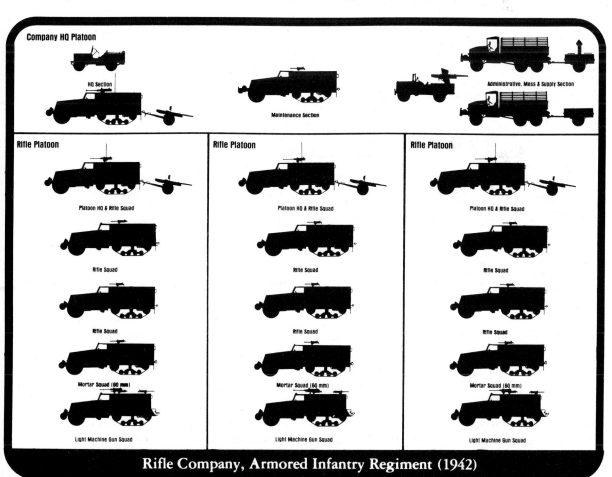

Rifle Company, Armored Infantry Regiment (1942)

(k) Occupy a defensive position.

(l) Perform reconnaissance and counter-reconnaissance.'

The normal attack formation for an armoured infantry company was two platoons in the assault, supported by the third rifle platoon and the AT platoon providing long-range cover. When confronting a weakly held position, all three rifle platoons would be used in the assault. Tactical doctrine called for the half-tracks to move forward until the infantry was forced—either by unfavourable terrain or by enemy fire—to dismount to carry on the attack. Against a town well defended by German infantry, the usual tactic was to send in a wave of tanks, followed closely by dismounted infantry, and finally the half-tracks with skeleton crews. If terrain was rough or snow covered the 'armoured doughs' would ride the tanks, half a squad per Sherman, as close to the objective as possible. Fire from moving half-tracks was officially discouraged as inaccurate and wasteful of ammunition; and mounted attack was not common when facing infantry, since a whole squad in the tight confines of a lightly armoured half-track was very vulnerable to a single grenade, mortar of Panzerfaust round. Mounted attacks were generally executed only against lightly held positions, or if there was an element of surprise where succeeding companies could mop up. Against small, demoralised German towns in the spring of 1945, mounted attacks were often effective.

The 'armoured dough' (or 'blitz dough', as

This M2A1 of the 495th Field Artillery, 12th Armd. Div. has been disabled by a German mine at Bining, France, on 12 October 1944. The distinctive feature of the M2/M2A1 was its internal stowage boxes, and this view clearly shows the outer access door. On this half-track a large stowage rack has been added to the rear. (US Signal Corps)

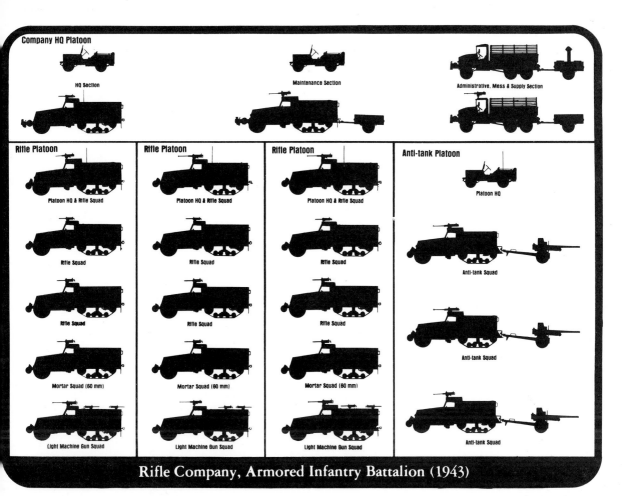

Company HQ Platoon

HQ Section

Maintenance Section

Administrative, Mess & Supply Section

Rifle Platoon

Platoon HQ & Rifle Squad

Rifle Squad

Rifle Squad

Mortar Squad (60 mm)

Light Machine Gun Squad

Rifle Platoon

Platoon HQ & Rifle Squad

Rifle Squad

Rifle Squad

Mortar Squad (60 mm)

Light Machine Gun Squad

Rifle Platoon

Platoon HQ & Rifle Squad

Rifle Squad

Rifle Squad

Mortar Squad (60 mm)

Light Machine Gun Squad

Anti-tank Platoon

Platoon HQ

Anti-tank Squad

Anti-tank Squad

Anti-tank Squad

Rifle Company, Armored Infantry Battalion (1943)

they were sometimes called), was spared of some of the foot-slogging misery of his 'straight-leg' infantry counterpart, but none of the sustained stress of combat. Because of their mobility, armoured infantry battalions could more easily be shifted to hot spots on the front, and so were often engaged in more prolonged combat than other units. 'Armoured doughs' soon learned to sleep in the awkward confines of their rattling half-tracks on night moves to new sectors. Casualties in armoured infantry battalions were disproportionately high due to their sustained, unrelieved combat duty. In a confidential report to the US Army Surgeon General on the subject of combat exhaustion it was pointed out that:

'In armoured divisions, with too few armoured infantry, the infantry contributes from 80 to 90 per cent of the [battle fatigue] casualties, rates becoming extremely high after third- to fifth-day actions. In hard, continued action, armoured infantry companies may be down to 40 to 50 men [from an original strength of 251 men], with three

company commanders being casualties in the process. One unit had 150 to 180 per cent replacements in 200 days; another, a 100 per cent turnover in 60 to 70 days.'

It was a common wisecrack in the infantry that you could tell an 'armoured dough' from a regular infantryman by the balding spot on the crown of his head. This was the result of too many leaps over the side of a half-track, with the helmet liner smacking against the wearer's skull. Armoured infantry half-tracks were likewise distinguished by their 'gypsy caravan' appearance. In France and Germany one of the most sought-after acquisitions for a squad was a small portable stove that could be moved into a barn when the squad bedded down for the night. Half-tracks soon became festooned with stovepipes, chairs, brooms, wash basins, pails, bed rolls and booty. The interior was full of more of the same, with sandbags on the floor to offer a little protection against mines, and an ill-gotten assortment of weaponry of American and German ancestry. The standard 'lootin' veer-

booten' rule was only discreetly enforced with regard to food and war trophies once the troops reached Germany. As an account of C Company, 17th AIB recalled: 'One advantage of dismounted attack was the opportunities for more thorough investigations of towns and the chance to fill in the deficiency of our K-ration diet.'

Comparison of infantry carriers

The M3 compared very favourably with the other main types of armoured personnel carriers used during World War II, the British Universal Carrier and the German SdKfz 251[1]. To supplement British production, the US manufactured 19,611 T16 Universal Carriers, but refused to use any, even for training. It was a 4-ton vehicle with even less armoured cover than the M3 half-track, was complicated and expensive, and could carry only four or five troops. The German SdKfz 251 half-track was very similar to the American half-track in terms of size, weight and road speed; but American troops who drove both distinctly preferred the American type. The M3 had over 20 per cent more internal capacity than the German half-track due to its box hull. The main advantage of the SdKfz 251 was its better armour layout. It had 8mm to 14mm of armour angled at 35°, while the American M3 had 6mm to 13mm at vertical or near-vertical angles. The main advantage of the M3 over the SdKfz 251 was much superior cross-country performance. Ground pressure of both vehicles was similar, but the M3 had over 25 per cent more horsepower and a powered front axle. The SdKfz 251 had an unpowered front axle, with a resultant loss of traction in poor terrain. It was nearly impossible to steer in mud or snow, and the complicated interleaved rear suspension became quickly impacted with mud and was difficult to keep maintained and lubricated. American trials of captured half-tracks found them prone to shed their tracks in rough terrain, and because they did not have a forward

[1]See Vanguard 32, *The SdKfz 251 Half-Track*.

An M3A1 of an infantry anti-tank squad of the 14th Armd. Div. passes the burned-out wreck of an M4A3(76mm)W knocked out the previous evening, 28 November 1944, by Tiger tanks during the fighting for Barre, France. Besides the prominent Allied star, the vehicle's name 'Baby Bastard No. 1' can be seen on the armoured radiator cover. (US Signal Corps)

roller bumper like the M3 or M2, embankments and terrain obstructions traversable by American half-tracks were impassable to the SdKfz 251.

Half-Tracks in Foreign Service

In 1942 the Army increased half-track requirements which necessitated selecting an additional manufacturer. The truck facilities of the International Harvester Company were chosen, and prototypes were built using components available at IHC, such as their RED-45-B engine. Two types were developed: the M5, which had a 13-seat capacity like the M3; and the M9, which had a ten-seat capacity like the M2. Although very similar in appearance to the M3 half-track, both the M5 and M9 had many distinct detail differences and dissimilar components. Most noticeable was the use of flat truck-style front fenders instead of the rounded automotive fenders of the M2 and M3.

Also, where the M2 and M3 had squared-off rear corners, on both the M5 and M9 the rear corners were rounded. Less apparent was the fact that the IHC M5s and M9s were manufactured from 7mm to 16mm homogeneous plate instead of the 6mm to 13mm face-hardened plate of the M2 and M3. Although the armour of the M5 and M9 was thicker, it offered marginally less ballistic protection. Production of the M5 began in December 1942, and 4,625 M5s were manufactured before production switched to the M5A1 in October 1943. The M5A1 corresponded to the M3A1, and incorporated the M49 pulpit mount and other automotive improvements. A total of 2,959 M5A1s were produced before manufacture ceased in March 1944. Production of the M9 began in March 1943 and ended in September 1943, with 2,026 M9s completed. The improved M9A1 was produced until December 1943, with 1,407 M9A1s completed. Unlike the M2 and M3, the IHC M5 and M9 are very difficult to distinguish externally. The M9 did not use exterior doors for access to the internal stowage boxes, it had the same rear door as the M5, and the hull did not have the noticeable difference in length of the M2/M3. The main difference between the M5 and M9 was internal stowage, and there was a very slight difference in the attachment of the external mine rack. In order to simplify logistics, the US Army decided to turn over most IHC half-tracks to Lend-Lease, and their only use by US forces was for training in the Continental US.

The largest recipient of American half-tracks was Britain, which received 5,690 M5s and M5A1s, and a large portion of M9 production. By the time that these vehicles began arriving in 1943 the British Army had standardised the Universal Carrier in the mechanised infantry rôle, and so American half-tracks were not used as extensively as troops carriers as in the US Army. They were employed in the motor battalions (equivalent to US AIBs) of some armoured formations in NW Europe in place of 15-cwt lorries, by the assault troops of recce regiments, and by the support troops of armoured car regiments. But it was more often as an armoured utility vehicle with Royal Engineer and Pioneer units, in HQ units, and as a prime mover for the 17pdr. and 6pdr. anti-tank guns that the half-track was seen.

The British Army turned over many of its half-tracks to other Commonwealth armies, most notably Canada, India and South Africa, and to the Free Polish forces, all of whom used them in the British fashion. The second largest user of American half-tracks was the French Army, which received at least 1,431 M3, M5 and M9 vehicles. The French followed American armoured infantry practices, and all three French armoured divisions that were committed to combat were equipped with US half-tracks. The Soviet Union received 342 M2, 2 M3, 401 M5 and 413 M9 half-tracks which were used almost exclusively in headquarters units of tank and other armoured formations. Half-tracks were also provided to the 1st Brazilian Infantry Division of the Brazilian Expeditionary Force, which fought in Italy: and to the Chinese, who used them in Burma.

Following the war, a large part of the US half-track inventory was declared surplus, and many vehicles were supplied to America's allies in Europe, South America and Asia. Some of these half-tracks are still in service, and Japan has only recently been retiring its half-tracks. Many half-tracks were sold in the US, where they were

M3A1 half-tracks of the 44th Armoured Inf. Bn., 6th Armd. Div rendevous in a field near Mageret, Belgium, during the Battle of the Bulge, 20 January 1945. (US Signal Corps)

This M2A1 photographed near Thionville, France, on 12 January 1945 shows the official engineer camouflage pattern for winter, breaking up the lime whitewash with strips of Olive Drab. (US Signal Corps)

stripped of their armour and the chassis used for heavy construction jobs, logging and auto repair and wrecking.

Probably the best known postwar combat use of American half-tracks was by the Israeli Zahal in the 1948, 1956, 1967 and 1973 wars. During the Palestine troubles the Israelis began buying surplus half-tracks in Europe and clandestinely shipping them to what would become Israel. While some remained unchanged and were used as infantry transporters, others were extensively modified, with heavy armament and even machine gun turrets[1]. In the 1950s, further shipments came

[1]See Vanguard 19, *Armour of the Middle East Wars 1948–78.*

from France. The basic troop carrier usually had a ball-mounted machine gun added in front of the squad leader station. Some were converted into tank destroyers with SS-11 wire-guided anti-tank missiles, and others were modified as mortar carriers. Indeed, the half-tracks had performed so well that in the late 1960s, when Gen. Avraham Adan attempted to modernise Zahal's armoured infantry with new M113s, he was firmly resisted by Gen. Israel Tal, commander of the Armoured Force. Nevertheless, Adan prevailed, and M113s gradually began to replace the half-track, though not completely by the time of the 1973 war. Following that war, half-tracks retired from armoured infantry duties were often rebuilt for use as command or engineer vehicles, or turned over to border security units. In the late 1970s a major modernisation programme was begun, adding a 6V53 engine (like that used in the M113), an Allison TX-100N automatic transmission and a Spicer gearbox. These vehicles have had their radiator louvres plated over, and have two large external fuel tanks added to the rear and covered with 10mm armour.

Half-Track Gun Carriages

Half-track Gun Motor Carriages

There were four basic categories of gun carriages based on the M3 half-track: GMC (Gun Motor Carriages) mainly used as tank destroyers, HMC (Howitzer Motor Carriages) used mainly as assault guns, MGMC (Multiple Gun Motor Carriages) used for air defence, and MMC or Mortar Motor Carriages.

The first gun motor carriage to enter development was the T12, which mated the M1897A4 75mm field gun to a standard M3 half-track chassis. This gun was a slightly modernised version of the famous old French 'soixante quinze'

and was chosen mainly because there was an ample supply of them available. The designers recognised from the start that this would be only a stop-gap tank destroyer, as armour cover was inadequate and gun traverse was very limited. It was accepted for service use in November 1941 as the 75mm GMC M3. The original batch used the same simple gun shield as the M2A3 gun carriage, but this was superseded in 1942 by a new shield which offered more protection for the crew. Production continued until April 1943, by which time 2,202 had been built. The last production batches used older M2A2 carriages as the stockpile of M2A3s had run out, and this version was called the 75mm GMC M3A1. (See also Vanguard 10, *Allied Tank Destroyers*.)

The first 50 of these vehicles were rushed to the Philippines, where they formed the three battalions of the Provisional Field Artillery Brigade. They

Heavily stowed M3A1s of the 23rd Armd. Engineers, 3rd Armd. Div. await orders to move out from the ruins of Duren, Germany, 26 February 1945. They are being shepherded by a single M-36 tank destroyer. (US Signal Corps)

A light machine gun squad of the 61st Armd. Inf. Bn. move forward through the German countryside on 17 April 1945. The half-track would appear to be an older M3 (winch) which has been rebuilt with an M49 ring mount and pulpit. Newly manufactured M3A1s had mine racks fitted to the hull side, which this vehicle, like many M3s, lacks. The half-track's armament includes both an air-cooled and a water-cooled .30cal. Browning. (US Signal Corps)

saw extensive fighting during the Bataan campaign, Capt. Gordon Peck's battery particularly distinguishing itself in support of the Provisional Tank Group. Back in the USA the new 75mm GMC M3s were being used to form the new tank destroyer battalions. The original TO&E called for eight 75mm GMC M3s, six 75mm GMC M5s and four 37mm GMC M6s. The M5 was an abominable design mounting a 75mm gun on a Cletrac airfield towing tractor. The Tank Destroyer Command called it the 'cleek-track', and refused to accept any for service use. The M6 was a ¾-ton Dodge truck with a 37mm gun mounted on the rear behind a thin armour shield. The 75mm GMC M3 took the place of the aborted M5, and the January 1943 TO&E change called for 36 M3s per battalion. During the fighting in North Africa five of the six tank destroyer battalions were equipped with the M3, there being only a handful of the new M10 tank destroyers available.

The 75mm GMC M3 was not a rousing success in Tunisia, in some cases because of improper employment. An Army Ground Force report candidly noted: '[The 601st and 701st TD Battalions] were generally used in rôles for which they were not designed such as infantry-accompanying guns, assault guns, assault artillery operating with tanks, and in cordon defence instead of in depth.' Nevertheless, when properly employed they could prove effective, as on 23 March 1943, when 31 M3s of the 601st TD Bn. repulsed over 100 German tanks attacking the 1st Infantry Division at El Guettar, knocking out 30 including two Tigers for a loss of 21 M3s. It is interesting to note that by this time the scantily armoured M6 had proved worthless in combat, and in the 601st TD Bn. and other units the 37mm gun was unbolted from the M6 and mounted in half-tracks as an improvised tank destroyer.

Although the 75mm GMC M3 served on during the fighting in Sicily, by this time it had largely been relegated to the fire support rôle since more M10 tank destroyers had become available. Although not extensively used by the US Army in Europe after the Sicilian campaign, except for training, the M3 and M3A1 GMCs continued to see action in the Pacific until the war's end. Each Marine Division had 12 of these in the Special Weapons Bn., where their firepower was much appreciated. They were used

1: M3 Command Vehicle, Maj.Gen.Patton, US I Armd. Corps, 1942

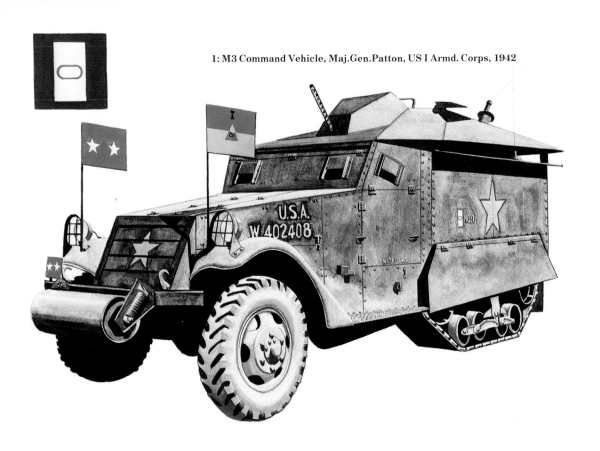

2: M2 37mm GMC, US 601st TD Bn.; Oran, Algeria, 1942

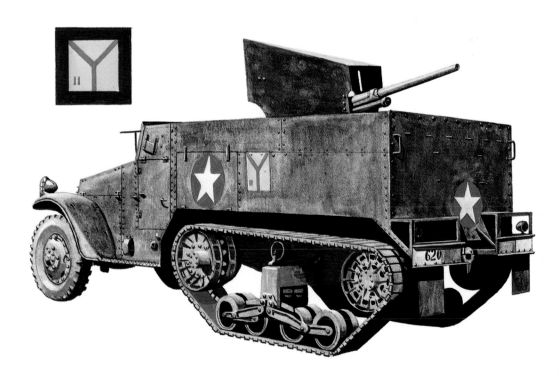

A

1: T19 105mm HMC, US 2nd Armd.Div.; Rabat, Morocco, Dec.1942

2: M3 Personnel Carrier, US 2nd Armd.Div.; Sicily, July 1943

1: T30 75mm HMC, US 1st Armd.Div.; Rabat, Morocco, July 1943

2: M3 Personnel Carrier, Brazilian Expeditionary Force; Italy, 1945

C

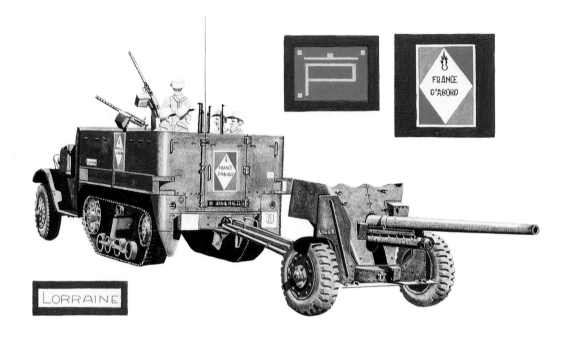

1: M9 Half-Track Armd. Car, RMLE, French 5^{e}DB; France, 1945

2: M5 Personnel Carrier, RMT, French 2^{e}DB; France, 1944

1: M3 75mm GMC, British 1st (King's) Dragoon Guards; Italy, 1944

2: M5 Personnel Carrier, 8th Bn. The Rifle Brigade, British 11th
   Armd.Div.;France, 1944

E

1: M16 MGC, 1st Lt.A-A Regt., Polish 1st Armd.Div.;France, 1944

2: M3 75mm GMC, 3rd US Marine Sp.Wpn. Bn.;Bougainville, 1943

1: M15A1 MGMC, 467th AAA Bn.; France, Dec. 1944

2: M16 MGMC, 447th AAA Bn.; Belgium, January 1945

G

1: SU-57 (T48 57mm GMC), Independent TD Bde., Soviet Army; Prague, 1945

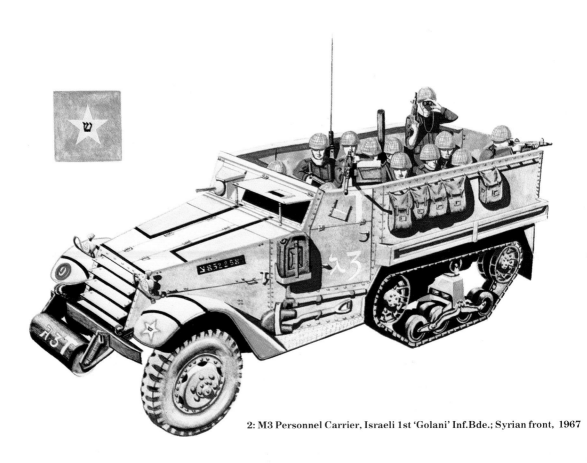

2: M3 Personnel Carrier, Israeli 1st 'Golani' Inf.Bde.; Syrian front, 1967

H

to attack bunkers and provide artillery support. Their only major anti-tank use came on Saipan, where they fought against the 9th Japanese Tank Regiment. Of the 2,202 M3s and M3A1s manufactured, 1,360 were later rebuilt as M3A1 half-track personnel carriers.

Britain was the only other country to receive the 75mm GMC M3 in any numbers. These were used mainly in the Heavy Troops of Armoured Car Regiments. The first unit to receive these was the Royal Dragoons, which had small numbers in Tunisia in 1943. They saw extensive use in Italy, and at least one troop remained in service during the fighting in France in 1944. Some were used by French troops in North Africa for training; and the Japanese captured at least one in the Philippines in 1942, where it greeted the US Army on its return in 1945.

The US Army intended to replace the 37mm anti-tank pop-gun with the British 6pdr., and so set about developing a tank destroyer version. The T44, which mounted the gun on a $\frac{3}{4}$-ton Ford light truck, was a failure, so it was decided to mount it on the ever-reliable half-track instead. This proved to be a straightforward conversion, and production was ready in December 1942. By May 1943, 962 had been built, but by this time experience in Tunisia made it clear that the 57mm GMC T48 was already obsolete. Thirty were supplied to Britain, where they were converted back to personnel carriers; 650 were supplied to the Soviet Union, and 281 were reconverted to M3 personnel carriers for the US Army. The

Chinese troops of the 1st Regt., 5332nd Bde. dismount from their M3 at Kabani, Burma, on 11 January 1945. The American star has been overpainted on the hull side and replaced with a circular unit insignia. This is the half-track of a light machine gun squad, judging from the two water-cooled Browning .30cal. weapons being dismounted. (US Signal Corps)

The personnel carrier version of the M3 half-track was not particularly common in the Pacific, its use being confined mainly to headquarters and maintenance units. This HQ vehicle took part in the fighting near a wrecked plant on Peleliu, Caroline Islands, in 1944. (US Signal Corps)

Soviet Union designated them SU-57, and used them from the summer of 1943 onwards in special independent tank destroyer brigades. These brigades had three battalions, totalling 60 SU-57s. Some were also supplied to Polish LWP units. The Soviet units remained in action until the end of the war.

Howitzer Motor Carriages

In October 1941 the Armored Force requested the crash development of a self-propelled mount for the 75mm field howitzer for use as an assault gun. As was the case with many of the gun and howitzer motor carriages, it was decided to design a quick field-expediency type on the M3 half-track which would be replaced by a more satisfactory vehicle when available. Ordnance developed a simple box frame on which to mount the M1A1 field howitzer, and it showed well in tests. It was accepted for service use in February 1942 as the 75mm HMC T30, and 500 were manufactured by November 1942. Like most

similar expedient vehicles, the fuel tanks were moved to the rear of the hull to provide more room around the gun, and ammunition stowage was provided in the floor. Anti-aircraft protection was provided by a .50cal. M2 machine gun mounted on a pedestal at the rear. The T30 first entered combat in North Africa in 1942. Each armoured regiment had 12: three in each tank battalion and three in the regimental reconnaissance battalion. Armoured infantry battalions each had nine: three per battalion. The infantry divisions fighting in North Africa each had a 'canon company' consisting of six 75mm HMC T30s and two 105mm HMC Y19s. The T30 remained in service through the Sicily and Italy campaigns, but never service in NW Europe, as the cannon company was dropped from infantry division organisation in March 1943 in favour of towed 105mm howitzers, and the new 75mm HMC M8 based on the M5A1 light tank gradually replaced it in armoured units. The last 108 T30s were remanufactured as M3 personnel carriers. Although no T30s served with US forces in the Pacific, the French used small numbers in Indo-China after the war.

At the same time as the T30 was requested by

the Armored Force, an urgent requirement was also expressed for a 105mm howitzer motor carriage. The designers were dubious about mounting an M2 105mm howitzer on a half-track, so they developed a version using the T7 pack howitzer as well. Surprisingly, the 105mm HMC T19 mounting the M2A1 howitzer proved successful, so the T38 mounting the T7 pack howitzer was dropped. Production of the T19 began in January 1942, and 324 were manufactured by April 1942. They were used to equip field artillery battalions in the armoured divisions and in the cannon companies of infantry divisions. The 105mm howitzer put a great deal of strain on the half-track chassis; but fortunately, during the course of the Tunisian campaign, the new 105mm HMC M7 Priest began to enter service, rendering the T19 a rather short-lived type. There was no export of the T19.

Multiple Gun Motor Carriages

There were numerous attempts to develop anti-aircraft versions of the M3 half-track for mobile protection of armoured columns, but only those which entered production are covered here. The most significant types were the family of vehicles mounting .50cal. M2 machine guns on Maxson

Foreign Légionnaires of the RMLE, 5ᵉ Division Blindée during the fighting in central France 1944. See also Plate D1. The stowage in the mine racks of this M9 half-track would appear to be fibreboard mortar round containers. Quite evident in this view is the colourful divisional insignia on the hull side, here with a green Legion grenade added, and the battalion insignia on the door: a yellow 'P' with two bars, one bearing the three 'stubs' of 3rd Co., 1st Bn. (ECPA)

turrets, and the M15 series armed with 37mm auto-cannons.

After several unsuccessful attempts to develop a machine gun anti-aircraft version of the M3 half-track, the W. L. Maxson Company submitted, in November 1941, designs for a novel self-powered turret mounting twin .50cal. machine gun. This M33 mount proved successful in trials, and was adapted for use on the M3, resulting in July 1942 in the M13 MGMC. The turret consisted of a seat for the gunner, two circular trunnion mounts for accurate gun aiming, a forward armoured shield for the gunner, and a small generator behind the gunner to permit power traverse and elevation for the gun even when the vehicle was static, without requiring the engine running to supply power. The success of the M13 in tests prompted the Army to request manufacture of an essentially similiar variant mounted

27

An M9 of an Indian Division tows a 17pdr. forward during the British 8th Army's attack on the Gustav Line in Italy near the Liri River, 12 May 1944. (Imperial War Museum)

Small numbers of half-tracks left over by the French were used by the South Vietnamese during the Vietnam War, like this M3 of the 1st ARVN Cav. Regt. sitting behind a protective burm. It is armed with M2 .50cal. and .30cal. machine guns behind improvised armour shields. (James Loop)

on the International Harvester M5. This became the M14 MGMC. A total of 1,103 M13s were manufactured by May 1943, as well as 1,600 M14s.

The entire production run of M14s was supplied to Britain, but as they were not readily compatible with British air defence doctrine most were converted back into personnel carriers. The M13 first entered service with the US Army in Italy in 1943, but its service life was short-lived. In the meantime, Ordnance had developed a modified Maxson turret with quad .50cal. machine guns, and this could be mounted in the M13 with little adaption. This was accepted for service use as the M16 in December 1942, and as in the case of the M13/M14, a similar M17 MGMC was based on the M5 half-track. A total of 2,877 M16s

were manufactured from May 1943 to March 1944, and in addition 677 M13s and 100 T10E1s were converted into M16s. The T10E1 was similar to the M13 but mounted twin 20mm cannon. However, the Army decided against adopting a calibre between .50 and 37mm, and the T10E1 was dropped.

The M16s became the standard US Army Light anti-aircraft vehicle in the fighting following the Normandy invasion. Each armoured division had an AAA Weapons Company with eight M16s and eight M15s. In addition, in June 1943, AAA Weapons Battalions (SP) began to be formed for use under Army-level command. Each had 32 M16s and 32 M15s in four auto-weapons battalions. These battalions were used to protect key bridges and other installations from air attack. The general absence of serious Luftwaffe opposition sometimes left the M16s free for the ground support rôle. Their enormous firepower earned them the grim nickname 'Meat-choppers'.

A number of 'expedient' M16s were made in the field by mounting towed Maxson turrets on M2 or M3 half-tracks. After the war, when many M3

The most prominent user of half-tracks after 1945 was the Israeli Army. They formed the backbone of the Zahal armoured infantry, only beginning to be replaced at the time of the 1973 war. They still remain in service in various rôles like this rebuilt M2 being used for border patrol. Like most of the rebuilt half-tracks, it has added rear fuel tanks besides automotive improvements such as the 6V53 diesel engine. (IDF)

personnel carriers were being retired from service, some were converted into M16A1s by adding a quad Maxson turret. Because these did not have the drop sides, the turret was mounted higher than on the ordinary M16. Most of these were supplied to Allied armies, and a later version had 'bat-wing' armour added to the turret to protect the ammunition handlers.

The M16 was used by the US Army in Korea; and the last reported employment was during the Newark riots in 1967 by National Guard units. It had long since been replaced in the Regular Army by the M42. The Israelis used several different versions of the .50cal. MGMCs in the Middle East wars, and in 1970 began replacing the .50cal. with twin HS 404 20mm cannons, resulting in the TCM-20. This version was credited with downing 60 per cent of the aircraft destroyed by Israeli ground air defences in the 1973 war. The entire production run of 1,000 M17s was supplied to the Soviet Union, where it was the most numerous armoured air defence vehicle available. It was warmly received, since the Soviets had no counterpart, and was also supplied to Polish LWP units.

In September 1941, APG began development of a Combination Gun Motor Carriage consisting of an M1A2 37mm auto-cannon and two water-cooled .50cal. machine guns on an M2 half-track. This was designated the T28, and while it was deemed acceptable by APG, the Coast Artillery

T30s of the US 2nd Armd. Div. take up firing positions near Licata, Sicily, during the fighting in 1943. Besides their main armament these vehicles each have a pair of .30cal. machine guns added on improvised mounts. They are camouflaged in a pattern of Olive Drab and Sand, common to most 2nd Armd. Div. vehicles on Sicily. The use of the circled star was first mandated for the Sicily operation to prevent inadvertent Allied air attack.

Board (which controlled Army anti-aircraft development) preferred a quad .50cal. system, so the T28 was dropped. In the summer of 1942, the Armored Force placed an urgent request for 80 anti-aircraft vehicles for use in the forthcoming North African invasion. The T28 project was re-

T19 105mm HMCs parade before Gen. George Patton and Gen. Nogues at a review on 19 December 1942 at Rabat, French Morocco. The T19 was quickly replaced by the M7 and saw significant combat action only during the fighting in Tunisia in 1943. (US Signal Corps)

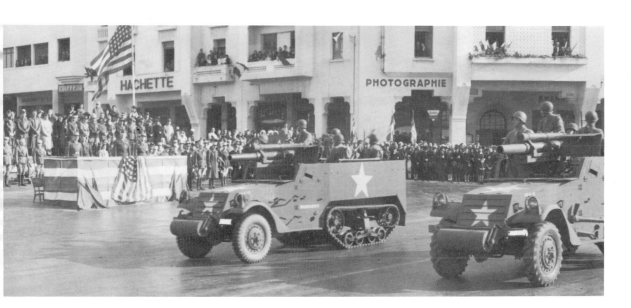

opened, and a modified version, the T28E1 on an M3 chassis, was accepted for production. Eighty were produced for service in Tunisia. They were credited with downing at least 78 enemy aircraft in a three-month period. An Army report indicated that one of the most successful tactics was to open fire with the machine guns first, to get the correct 'lead'. On some occasions the tracer stream misled German pilots into underestimating the range of the guns, and when it came nearer, it was easily destroyed by the longer-ranged 37mm auto-cannon.

The T28E1 MGMC offered no protection for its crew, so when it was type-classified as the M15 MGMC in 1943 a simple box armour shield was designed. A further 600 were built until April 1943, when it was decided to modify the mount and introduce other improvements based on experiences in Tunisia and Italy. Production of this version, the M15A1, began in October 1943, and by February 1944, 1,652 were manufactured. The M15 and the M15A1 were almost identical in appearance, the M15 having the .50cal. machine guns above the main gun, and the M15A1 below. The M15 was used in conjunction with M16s in the AAA Weapons Companies and Battalions, as mentioned earlier. An interesting field variation of the M15 was made by the Coopers Plains 99th Ordnance Depot in Australia,

The troops of mortar companies of the 41st Armd. Inf., 2nd Armd. Div. were not happy with the standard configuration of the M4 81mm mortar carrier, which had the mortar pointed rearward only. They rebuilt their vehicles to permit the tube to fire forward, as shown in this view of an M4A1. An aiming stake can be seen on the lip of the engine cover near the stencilled 'Prestone' marking (this marking refers to the addition of anti-freeze to the vehicle radiator). The national insignia is the uncommon white star on blue surround. This particular vehicle was photographed in England on 12 April 1944 before the division was committed to the Normandy fighting. (US Signal Corps)

where a 40mm Bofors was substituted for the usual armament. Official development of such a vehicle had been dropped because of heavy gun recoil, and the desirability of the new M19 twin 40mm MGMC. However, in the Pacific the M16s and M15s were often used in the ground support rôle, where the heavier fire of the 40mm was very desirable. Eighteen of these were built, and they fought with the 209th AAA Battalion on Luzon in 1945. Quite surprisingly, the vehicles were refurbished during the Korean War and used again, finally being turned over to South Korean forces after the war. The Soviet Union received 100 M15s, and many M15s and M15A1s were supplied to America's allies after the war, notably to Japan.

Mortar Carriers

The 81mm Mortar Carrier M4 was among the earliest versions of the M2 half-track, being standardized in October 1941. The M4 mounted an M1 mortar which fired over the rear of the vehicle. There was a skate ring mounted on the floor which provided limited traverse. Through 1942, 572 were manufactured. These were used in armoured regiments, where there were three in the HQ company of each tank battalion; in armoured infantry regiments there were four in the HQ company of each infantry battalion. On the M4 the mortar was actually intended to be used from the vehicle only in emergency, and normally from a ground emplacement. In 1943 an improved version was developed, the M4A1, which increased the traverse of the mortar and improved the mount to permit firing from the vehicle without

Although the M6 tank destroyer proved worthless in combat, a number of units stripped the 37mm gun mount from M6s converted back to three-quarter-ton trucks, and mounted it in half-tracks, like this M2, 'Rough Rider II' of the 41st Armd. Inf., 2nd Armd. Div. (US Signal Corps)

An M3 75mm GMC of the 1st (King's) Dragoon Guards near Montecero, Italy, 1944. The 75mm GMC M3s were used in heavy troops of armoured car regiments in Italy to provide fire support. (Imperial War Museum)

harm to the chassis. Between March 1942 and October 1943 600 M4A1s were manufactured. Some of the units using the M4 and M4A1 were unhappy about the rear firing configuration. The 2nd Armored Division modified its vehicles to permit forward firing. This view was recognised by Ordnance, which developed a new mortar

An SU-57 (T48 57mm Gun Motor Carriage) of a Soviet tank destroyer brigade drives past a crowd of jubilant Czechs following the liberation of Prague in May 1945. (Sovfoto)

carrier which could fire forward. Unlike the M4 and M4A1 the new 81mm Mortar Carrier M21 was based on the M3 half-track. Although there was more internal space in the M21, it carried only one more round of ammunition—97—than the earlier M4A1. Only 110 M21s were manufactured between January and March 1944, of which 54 were supplied to the French. Few other mortar carriers were exported, although Zahal developed a very successful mortar carrier version of the M3 using the 120mm Soltam.

The Plates

A1: M3 Command Vehicle, Maj.Gen. George S. Patton, US I Armored Corps; Desert Training Center, 1942.

Although Patton's penchant for personalised uniforms and ivory-handled revolvers is well known, he also had an affection for customised armoured command vehicles. While in command of the Desert Training Center on the California/Nevada border in 1942, he had this M3 half-track

with an added armoured roof and other modifi-
cations. In May 1942 he wrote to Eisenhower,
McNair (head of the AGF) and others urging that
the Army adopt a system of marking vehicles to
facilitate unit identification. His own half-track,
'Nite-owl', carried this white rectangular insignia
followed by HQ-1. The symbol is obviously
derived from the Army map symbol for an
armoured unit. This insignia was repeated on the
left hull rear bumper with the right bumper
bearing the numbers 'I-56' opposite in yellow.
The national insignia, in keeping with the January
1942 Armored Force order calling for the use of Air
Corps Yellow No. 4 Lusterless for markings, are
painted in yellow on the hull sides, front and rear
and on the engine deck. Also prominent are the
sheet metal pennants for a major general on the
right, and for 1st Armored Corps on the left. This
vehicle was left behind at the Desert Training
Center when Patton was assigned to North
Africa, where he used an M3A1 Scout Car with
added armour shields.

Eighty T28E1s were hastily manufactured to provide air
cover for American tank units in Tunisia in 1943, where they
proved quite successful. Like many American armoured
vehicles during the campaign, this half-track is camouflaged
by application of light coloured mud.

An M3 75mm GMC of the Special Weapons Bn., 2nd Marine
Div. in action on Tinian, 30 July 1944. The fibreboard packing
containers for its 75mm gun ammunition litter the ground
around the vehicle. (US Marine Corps)

A2: M2 37mm Gun Motor Carriage, US 601st Tank
  Destroyer Battalion; Oran, 1943

The M6 37mm Gun Motor Carriage, a tank destroyer consisting of a 37mm gun mounted on a ¾-ton Dodge 4 × 4 light truck, was so unpopular among the troops that in some units the gun and shield were removed and remounted in half-tracks to provide more mobility and armour. This particular conversion served with the 601st TD Bn. of the 1st Armored Division. The use of Air Force style national insignia was called for in a GHQ MEF order to all US forces committed to the Mediterranean theatre on 31 August 1942. Nevertheless, the order was widely ignored, with most vehicles either retaining the yellow Armored Force stars, or the standard white US Army stars. The 'II' on the yellow and red battalion insignia presumably refers to the 2nd Company. Note also that the extremities of the rear bumperettes have been painted white for increased visibility. The national insignia was also painted on the hood (36ins. diameter) and on the radiator louvres (20ins. diameter). Like all US Army half-tracks, this vehicle is finished in overall No. 9 Olive Drab.

B1: T19 105mm Howitzer Motor Carriage, US 2nd
  Armored Division; Rabat, 20 December 1942

During Operation 'Torch', many American vehicles had the US flag painted on the hull side in the vain hope that the French would not fire on American troops. This vehicle also carries the Armored Force yellow stars, even though in December 1942 orders were issued to revert back to white stars, since the yellow markings tended to become obscured by dust. It's interesting to note that other T19s participating in the 20 December Franco-American review at Rabat had the later style markings, dropping the flag insignia and using white stars. It is not clear which battalion this vehicle belonged to, as the bumper codes '3 5 F/E-24' are believed to have been intentionally spurious for counter-intelligence reasons. The vehicle did belong to E Battery, however, as is evident both from the bumper code and the vehicle name 'Evelyn'. The vehicle serial number is hardly evident due to the use of blue-drab paint. Although blue-drab paint was first developed and employed in 1940 to make serial numbers and other markings less conspicuous, the change in

A veteran T28E1 of the 443rd AAA Bn. guards an airfield at St. Raphael in southern France on 17 August 1944, shortly after the invasion. Unlike the standardised M15, the T28E1 was without a rear armour shield, and used water-cooled .50cal. machine guns. (US Signal Corps)

An M15 drives off an LCT behind an M8 scout car during the invasion of southern France, 15 August 1944. This vehicle already has ample claimed aircraft kills registered on the side of the 37mm ammunition box forward of the turret, presumably scored in Italy. (US Signal Corps)

Army Regulation 850-5 did not officially come about until June 1942. This style remained in effect until a regulation change in February 1945, when it reverted back to white. In fact, all through the war serial numbers were often painted in white since this paint was available for national insignia and unit bumper codes, while the blue-drab was seldom to be found except in the factories.

B2: M3 Personnel Carrier, US 2nd Armored Division; St. Stefano, Sicily, 19 July 1943

On 9 March 1943, Allied Force HQ issued Operational Memorandum #34 regarding camouflage painting of US vehicles in anticipation of Operation 'Husky', the invasion of Sicily. It called for the use of sprayed disruptive patterns of either No. 6 Earth Yellow or No. 8 Earth Red on all combat vehicles. Patterns were supplied, but the orders called for variation in the design, and stressed the use of horizontal rather than vertical patterns. The vehicles of the 2nd Armored Division were spray-camouflaged with Earth Yellow, like the M3 shown here. Also, on 3 July 1943, AFHQ signalled its units: 'For urgent operational reasons, all vehicles for 'Husky' which have white stars will have circles widened to at least double the present size. Yellow paint to be used if possible. If not, then white, blue or red in that order of priority.' This vehicle used an enlarged white circle which ran over the edge of

the engine deck hood, as is shown in the inset drawing. Some vehicles in the 2nd Armored Division had even thicker circular rims, sometimes in yellow. The reason for the adoption of the circle for the Sicily operation was that Allied fighter-bomber pilots had complained that at a distance the US star could be mistaken for a white cross. The bumper code on this vehicle was '2Δ41-I/B-29' which indicated a vehicle of B Company, 1st Battalion, 41st Armored Infantry Regiment. Since 1941 2nd Armored Division had used a system of geometric symbols which were carried under the vehicle name. Although the entire system is not known, the symbol on this vehicle is repeated in detail on the inset drawing.

C1: T30 75mm Howitzer Motor Carriage, US 1st Armored Division, Rabat, 4 July 1943

During the course of the Tunisian fighting the 1st Armored Division was obliged to use mud to camouflage their vehicles. While the division was recuperating in the Rabat area in the summer of 1943, regular US Army Engineer paint became available, and prior to the 4 July parade in honour of US Independence Day the vehicles participating in the parade were 'spiffed up' by camouflage-painting them in Olive Drab and No. 3 Sand, as shown here.

C2: M3 Personnel Carrier, Brazilian Expeditionary Force; Italy, 1945
The Brazilian Expeditionary Force was equipped entirely with US equipment and uniforms during the fighting in Italy. Its vehicles usually used the Brazilian national insignia in place of the US star, carrying them in the same location and in roughly the same size as shown here. This was repeated on the hood and on the radiator louvres.

D1: M9 Half-Track Armored Car, Régiment de Marche de la Légion Etrangère, 5ᵉ Division Blindée, Alsace, 1945
This Foreign Legion half-track carries the full set of 5ᵉ DB insignia. The divisional patch with the 'France d'Abord' motto and Legion grenade was carried on the rear, both hull sides and on the

hood. The regimental patch was carried on the left rear, and on both the driver's and opposite doors. The 'P' indicates the regiment; the bar indicates 2ᵉ Bn. by its position, and the second company of that battalion by the vertical 'stub'; and the dots indicate the 3ᵉ Peleton. The vehicle name 'Lorraine' is carried on the hull side, and the name 'Lille' is carried on the M1 57mm anti-tank gun shield. The bumperettes have been painted white for visibility, as were the outer portions of the front bumper. The underlined red '30' on the right bumperette indicates the vehicle's maximum road speed.

D2: M5 Personnel Carrier, RMT, 2ᵉ Division Blindée, Alençon, France, August 1944
This half-track of the Régiment de Marche du Tchad carries its name, 'Mercantour', above the radiator louvres, and has the circular divisional patch and national insignia on each hull side. The vehicle serial number is carried front and rear preceded by national colours, and a pennant is flown attached to the winch/bumper girder. The 2ᵉ DB used a marking system like that of 5ᵉ DB, and for this vehicle it would logically have been a

An M15A1 of the 2nd Anti-aircraft Artillery stands watch at Machinato, Okinawa, on 12 June 1945. While the M15 had the two .50cal. machine guns located above the main 37mm gun, on the M15A1 the machine guns were below. (US Signal Corps)

Lacking much air opposition during the Luzon campaign, M16s were often used for ground support, like this 'Meat-Chopper' of the 209th AAA Bn. supporting tanks of the 754th Tank Bn. near Kiangan, 13 July 1945. (US Signal Corps)

white or yellow 'B' on a pale blue square, though this vehicle seems to lack it. The 2ᵉ DB usually used the Allied star for air recognition, as is the case with this vehicle.

E1: M3 75mm Gun Motor Carriage, The King's Dragoon Guards; Cassino area, Italy, 20 February 1944.

This vehicle is finished in overall Olive Drab with a pattern of Light Mud paint. It is from the Heavy Troop of B Sqn., and carries the B Sqn. square as well as the name 'Belching Bella' on the gun recuperator housing. The red/white/red British Army AFV recognition sign is prominent on the hull side and is shown on the inset drawing.

E2: M5 Personnel Carrier, 8th Bn. The Rifle Brigade, British 11th Armoured Division; France, August 1944

This vehicle carries the divisional insignia to the left, the 'B' Co. square and platoon number in the centre, and the battalion's unit code flash to the right on the hull rear. These insignia, except for the company square, would be repeated on the front bumper, while the company insignia is carried on the hull side. The vehicle serial begins with 'Z', indicating a personnel carrier. The hull star is without the circle, but that on the hood would

carry a circle. This vehicle was much more heavily stowed than illustrated here, but is shown free of all the kit so as to illustrate the markings clearly.

F1: M16 Multiple Gun Carriage, 1 Pulk artylerii przeciwlotniczej lekkiej, 1 Dywizja Pancerna, France 1944

This M16 carries the insignia of the 1st Polish Armoured Division on the left mudguard, the regimental unit code flash (a white '73' on a red/blue square) on the right mudguard and a bridging circle in the centre of the winch/bumper assembly. On the hull side is the Allied star, and forward of this a typical British-style artillery marking. The location of the red square in the upper right corner indicates 1st Battery, while the 'B3' indicates sub-unit. This insignia, along with the aforementioned markings, were repeated on the two rear stowage boxes as shown in the inset drawing. The 'PL' in a white oval was used on some Polish vehicles for national identification. The vehicle is finished overall in a 'Mickey Mouse' pattern of Olive Drab and black.

An M16 and M15 Special of the 209th AAA Bn. support the 32nd Inf. Div. during fighting on the Villa Verde Trail in the Philippines, August 1945. The M15 Special was a field-modified half-track with a 40mm Bofors instead of the usual 37mm gun. (US Signal Corps)

F2: M3 75mm Gun Motor Carriage, US 3rd Marines Special Weapons Battalion; Bougainville, 1943

This vehicle was one of 12 attached to the Special Weapons Bn. of the 3rd Marine Division on Bougainville. Each of the Marine Divisions had a geometric marking which was occasionally used on vehicles as well as uniforms, a diamond being used by the 3rd Marine Division. In some cases the letters SW were carried inside this marking (for Special Weapons Battalion); or, as in this case, a code number. There was no standardisation of camouflage painting in this unit, some vehicles having this pattern of No. 1 Light Green over No. 9 Olive Drab with black edging, but others having no camouflage pattern painting at all.

G1: M15A1 Multiple Gun Carriage, US 467th AAA Battalion; Sedan, France, 27 December 1944

As was the case with most American armoured vehicles in France, this M15A1 is in monotone No. 9 Olive Drab. Its insignia consist of standard white bumper codes '1A 467AAA/D31' at front and rear, and the crew's personal insignia, a green dragon with yellow trim. This vehicle also carried a 36in. diameter air identification star, with surround, on the hood.

G2: M16 Multiple Gun Carriage, US 447th AAA Battalion, Neufchâteau, Belgium, 1 January 1945

It's interesting to note that this M16 retained its summer camouflage of No. 9 Olive Drab with a disruptive pattern of No. 10 Black even during the Battle of the Bulge in snowy Belgium. These patterns were usually sprayed by engineer units, as armoured units seldom had the paint, equipment or inclination to do it themselves. Stowage racks for additional German jerry cans have been added next to the winch, and the air identification star and serial are painted in white. No bumper codes are evident.

H1: SU-57 (T48 57mm Gun Motor Carriage) of a Soviet Independent Tank Destroyer Brigade; Prague, 1945

The Russians seldom bothered to repaint Lend-Lease equipment like this SU-57, or even to over-paint the blue-drab serial number and national identification. Indeed, in Eastern Europe in 1944–45, the USA markings on Lend-Lease trucks and armoured vehicles were so widely seen that common folk wisdom explained it to mean 'Ubiyat Sukinsyna Adolfa' ('Kill that son-of-a-bitch Adolf'), since the Russians were loath to acknowledge where this equipment came from. The brigade insignia, a yellow '36' in a diamond, was carried on the hull side along with the vehicle tactical number, and both were repeated on the right rear stowage box. The white triangle was the May 1945 air-identification marking for the Soviet Army.

An anti-aircraft unit of the Soviet 4th Mechanised Corps in Hungary in 1945 equipped with Lend–Lease M3A1 Scout Cars and M17 MGMCs. Aside from 100 M15s, the 1000 M17s supplied to the Soviet Union by the US were the only armoured, mechanised air defence equipment available to the Soviets. (Sovfoto)

M16s were extensively used in Korea for ground support, like this vehicle of the 92nd AAA Bn., 1st Cavalry defending a bridge below Tabu Dong, 6 September 1950. (US Signal Corps)

OLD EXPENDABLE

H2: M3 Personnel Carrier, Israeli 1st 'Golani' Infantry Brigade; Syrian Front, June 1967

Like most Israeli half-tracks, this vehicle is finished in overall 'sand grey' and has had a machine gun position added to the right of the driver. The white 'T' with black edging is an air identification insignia carried on Israeli trucks and half-tracks in 1967. The bar extended down the rear of the vehicle as well, more or less covering the rear access door. The vehicle serial is painted in black with white lettering on the hood side. The Hebrew letter *gimel* and number '3' indicate the third vehicle of the third platoon, and the white 'T' on the door is presumably a company insignia. These insignia are repeated on the front roller. On the right fender is the standard Israeli blue and red bridging circle (giving the vehicle weight of 9 tons maximum); and on the left is an insignia of the Hewbrew letter *sin* in a white star, possibly signifying the 'Golani' Brigade.

Notes sur les planches en couleur

A1 Véhicule modifié selon les desiderata du General Patton, ainsi que les marquages, quand il commandait le centre d'entraînement en désert, en Californie en 1942. Notez les fanions en métal du général de division et *I Corps*. On a imposé les marquages jaunes pour les blindés à partir de janvier 1942. **A2** L'insigne national de l'Aviation fut imposé aux troupes en Méditerranée en août 1942 mais beaucoup de véhicules gardèrent leurs étoiles jaunes ou blanches. Des étoiles de 90cm et de 50cm de diamètre étaient aussi peintes sur le capot du moteur et sur le radiateur, respectivement. Le 'II' sur l'insigne de Bataillon rouge et jaune identifie probablement la *2nd Company*.

B1 Le drapeau national devait être peint pour l'opération 'Torche'; ici, les étoiles nationales jaunes règlementaires antérieures ont été remplacées par des blanches en décembre 1942. Le nom du véhicule, 'Evelyn', indique qu'il était en service avec la *E Battery* mais il est inconnu car il est très possible que les marquages sur les pare-chocs aient été délibérément falsifiés pour tromper les services secrets ennemis. **B2** Véhicule de la *B Company, 41st Armored Infantry Regt., 1st Batalion*—voyez les marquages de pare-chocs. Les trainées jaune-terre de camouflage et le grand cercle autour de l'étoile nationale furent imposés pour l'invasion de la Sicile.

C1 La peinture *Olive Drab* et *Sand* de camouflage fut appliquée avant le défilé de l'Independence Day de cette date. Avant cela, les véhicules de cette division étaient obligés d'utiliser la boue. **C2** Equipement et couleurs américaines avec un insigne national brésilien remplaçant l'étoile US partout, y compris le capot et le radiateur.

D1 Insigne de la Division avec la grenade de la Légion ajoutée à l'arrière, sur les côtés et sur le capot. La lettre du régiment, 'P' avec lignes et points identifie le 2ème Bataillon, 2ème Compagnie, 3ème Peloton. Notez que les noms sont différents sur le véhicule et le canon en remorque. **D2** Insigne de division sur les deux côtés de la caisse, avec le fanion tricolore.

E1 Le fanion rouge et blanc identifiait les blindés anglais; et le carré bleu de *B Squadron* ce régiment. Ces canons étaient utilisés par les *Heavy Troops* de chaque *Squadron*. **E2** De gauche à droite, les marquages sont ceux de la Division; de la *6 Troop; B Squadron*. Le numéro de code identifie le régiment de la division.

F1 Les garde-boue portent le numéro de code d'unité du régiment et l'insigne de division. Le marquage sur le côté de la caisse identifie la *1st Battery* du régiment de la façon habituelle à l'artillerie anglaise et 'B3' identifie ce véhicule au sein de la *Battery* et la *Troop*. **F2** Le marquage en losange et '105' sont des marquages codés pour le *Battalion* de cette *Division*. Au sein de l'unité, les camouflages étaient très divers.

G1 A part le dragon, insigne personnel de l'équipage, ce véhicule porte les marquages standard de l'armée US. **G2** Notez que le camouflage d'été olive et noir a été conservé, même dans la neige des Ardennes.

H1 Insigne de brigade soviétique, '36' dans un losange sur le côté de la caisse, avec le numéro du véhicule. Les unités russes prenaient rarement la peine de repeindre le matériel fourni par les Américains. **H2** Peinture gris-sable standard des Israéliens. Le marquage blanc en 'T' bordé de noir sur le dessus et à l'arrière du véhicule sont pour la reconnaissance aérienne. Le marquage *Gimel 3* identifie le 3ème véhicule du 3ème Peloton et la Pettre *Sin* sur fond d'étoile indique probablement la brigade.

Farbtafeln

A1 Persönlich modifiziertes Fahrzeug und persönlich ausgedachte Markierungen von Gen. Patten, als er das Wüstentrainingscenter in Californien im Jahr 1942 kommandierte. Die Markierungen der gepanzerten Fahrzeuge wurden von Januar 1942 an in gelb angeordnet. **A2** Luftwaffen-Nationalabzeichen wurden für die Truppen im Mittelmeerraum vom August 1942 an angeordnet, jedoch behielten viele Fahrzeuge das gelbe oder weisse Sternenabzeichen. Sterne von einem Durchmesser von 36 zoll und 20 zoll waren auch oben auf die Motorenhaube und beziehungsweise vorne auf den Kühler gemalt. Das 'II' auf dem rot und gelben Bataillonsabzeichen identifiziert wahrscheinlich die 2. Kompanie.

B1 Nationale Fahnenmarkierungen wurden für die Operation 'Torch' angeordnet; hier werden auch die gelben nationalen Sterne von früheren Anordnungen getragen, obwohl so angeordnet, wurden sie im Dezember 1943 durch weisse ersetzt. Der Fahrzeugname 'Evelyn' zeigt an, dass es mit 'E Battery' diente, jedoch ist dessen Einheit andererseits unbekannt, da man glaubt, dass die Markierungen an den Stosstangen absichtlich 'gefälscht' wurden, um den feindlichen Nachrichtendienst zu täuschen. **B2** Fahrzeug der 'B Company, 41st Armored Infantry Regt., 1st Battalion'—siehe Stosstangenmarkierungen. Die erdgelben Tarnungsschmierer und der weite Kreis um den Nationalstern wurden beide für die Sizilien-Invasion angeordnet.

C1 'Olive Drab' und 'Sand' Tarnfarbe wurde vor der Unabhängigkeitsparade dieses Datums gezwungen, Lehm als Tarnung zu benutzen. **C2** Amerikanische Ausrüstung und Farbschema mit dem brasilianischen Nationalabzeichen den US-Stern in allen Positionen ersetzend, einschliesslich oben auf der Motorhaube und vorne am Kühler.

D1 Das Divisionsabzeichen mit der Granate der Legion hinzugefügt, wird hinten, an beiden Seiten und oben auf der Motorhaube getragen. Der Regimentsbuchstabe 'P' mit Streifen und Punkten identifiziert 2. Bataillon, 2. Companie, 3. Zug. Bemerke die unterschiedlichen Namen am Fahrzeug und dem gezogenen Geschütz. **D2** Divisionsabzeichen an beiden Rumpfseiten mit nationalem Trikoloenanstrich.

E1 Das rot und weisse Erkennungszeichen identifizierte britische Panzerfahrzeuge; das blaue Quadrat, 'B Squadron' dieses Regiments. Diese Geschütze dienten mit dem 'Heavy Troop' jeden Schwadrons. **E2** Die Markierungen von links nach rechts sind das Divisionsabzeichen; das Abzeichen des 6 Troop, B Squadron; und die Codenummer identifiziert das Regiment innerhalb der Division.

F1 Die Kotflügel tragen die Einheitscodenummer des Regiments und das Divisionsabzeichen. Die Rumpfseitenmarkierungen identifizieren die 1st Battery des Regiments in der üblichen Art der britischen Artillerie; und 'B3' identifiziert das Fahrzeug innerhalb der 'Battery' und 'Troop'. **F2** Die rautenförmige Markierung und '105' sind chiffrierte Abzeichen für dieses 'Battalion' innerhalb dieser Division. Tarnfarben innerhalb dieser Einheit variierten weitgehend.

G1 Abgesehen von dem persönlichen Abzeichen eines Drachens der Mannschaft hat dieses Fahrzeug totale einheitliche US Armee-Markierungen. **G2** Bemerke die Sommertarnfarbe von oliverfarben und schwarz, selbst im Schnee der Ardennen zurückbehalten.

H1 Sowjetisches Brigadenabzeichen, '36' in einer Raute an der Rumpfseite, mit der Fahrzeugnummer. Sowjetische Einheiten nahmen sich selten die Mühe, amerikanisch gelieferte Ausrüstung neu anzumalen. **H2** 'Sandgraues' israelisches Grundfarbenschema; weisse 'T'-förmige Markierungen zur Luftwaffenerkennung, in schwarz eingefasst, oben und hinten am Fahrzeug; die Markierung 'Gimel 3' identifiziert das dritte Fahrzeug des 3. Zuges, und der Buchstabe 'Sin' auf einem Stern identifiziert vermutlich die Brigade.